# Yucky Riddles

## Marilyn Helmer

## Eric Parker

Kids Can Press

What would you call Batman and Robin if they were run over by a speeding train?

Splatman and Ribbon

Why did the witch dye her hair green?

So it would match her teeth

What kind of sandwich would you never want to eat?

Peanut butter and jellyfish

What did the tiger say when he felt sick to his stomach?

Maybe it was someone I ate.

What would you get if you crossed a mosquito with a lollipop?

A bloodsucker

Why is your nose the most unpopular part of your face?

Because it smells

What is the best way to talk to a monster with bad breath?

By telephone

What kind of bug makes your nose run?

A flu bug

What goes *ha, ha, ha, plop?*

Someone laughing their head off

Where should you save your toenail clippings?

In a nail-file, of course!

What do you sing when the birthday girl gets sick at her party?

Happy Barf-day to you!

# What is a cannibal's favorite vegetable?

Human beans

What do you call a baby skunk?

A little stinker

Why did the cookie turn green?

It was feeling crummy.

What's worse than picking your nose?

Picking someone else's

What do you get if you cross a large green fruit with a toad?

A wart-ermelon

What kind of brush should you never use on your hair?

Your toothbrush

What should you give a gorilla with an upset stomach?

Lots of room!

Is it okay to eat french fries with your fingers?

No, you should save your fingers for dessert!

What kind of ball should you never play soccer with?

An eyeball

What's worse than finding a worm in your sandwich?

Finding half a worm

What should you say to a skeleton with a wart on the end of its nose?

Nothing — skeletons don't have noses.

Which bug is always on time?

A clock-roach

# What is the daily special at the Doggie Diner?

Fleasburgers

# What has six legs and drools?

Triplets

Why did the boy think he was upside down?

Because his nose was running and his feet smelled

# Which kind of ice cream makes you sick?

Van-ill-a

What animal has two horns, four legs and flies?

A dead cow

What's worse than an elephant with bad breath?

A centipede with stinky feet

What did the rooster say when he stepped in horse manure?

Cock-a-doodle-poo!

**For Dorothy, who loves a Yucky chuckle! — M.H.**

Kids Can Read is a trademark of Kids Can Press

Text © 2003 Marilyn Helmer
Illustrations © 2003 Eric Parker

Kids Can Press acknowledges the financial support of the Ontario Arts
Council, the Canada Council for the Arts and the Government of Canada,
through the BPIDP, for our publishing activity.

Published in Canada by        Published in the U.S. by
Kids Can Press Ltd.           Kids Can Press Ltd.
29 Birch Avenue               2250 Military Road
Toronto, ON  M4V 1E2          Tonawanda, NY  14150

www.kidscanpress.com

Edited by David MacDonald
Designed by Stacie Bowes and Marie Bartholomew
Printed in Hong Kong, China, by Book Art Inc., Toronto

The hardcover edition of this book is smyth sewn casebound.
The paperback edition of this book is limp sewn with a drawn-on cover.

CM 03  0 9 8 7 6 5 4 3 2 1
CM PA 03  0 9 8 7 6 5 4 3 2 1

**National Library of Canada Cataloguing in Publication Data**

Helmer, Marilyn
    Yucky riddles / Marilyn Helmer, Eric Parker.

(Kids Can read)
ISBN 1-55337-448-7 (bound).     ISBN 1-55337-414-2 (pbk.)

1. Riddles, Juvenile. I. Parker, Eric  II. Title.  III. Series:
Kids Can read (Toronto, Ont.)

PN6371.5.H449 2003        jC818'.5402        C2002-904612-2

Kids Can Press is a /ᵒⲅⴞS™ Entertainment company